Walking Sticks

The World's Longest Insects

by Leon Gray

Consultant: Peter Smithers
School of Biomedical & Biological Sciences
University of Plymouth, England

BEARPORT
PUBLISHING

New York, New York

Credits

Cover, © Patricio Robles Gil/Nature Picture Library; 2–3, © Dr. Morley Read/Shutterstock; 4–5, © Natural History Museum, London/ Science Photo Library; 6–7, © Chris & Tilde Stuart/FLPA; 8, © Natural History Museum, London/Science Photo Library; 10–11, © Dr. Morley Read/Shutterstock; 12, © Dja65/Shutterstock; 13, © Xander Fotografie/Shutterstock; 14, © Sandrien/Shutterstock; 15, © Jean Paul Ferrero/ Ardea; 16, © Chien Lee/Minden Pictures/FLPA; 17, © Patricio Robles Gil/naturepl.com; 18, © Natural History Museum, London/Science Photo Library; 19, © Imagebroker/Christian Haltter/FLPA; 20, © Anthony Bannister/Gallo Images/Corbis; 21, © Peter MacDiarmid/Reuters/ Corbis; 22L, © Drägü/Wikipedia; 22C, © Malcolm Schuyl/FLPA; 22R, © Nick Gordon/Ardea; 23TL, © Dr. Morley Read/Shutterstock; 23TR, © Chien Lee/Minden Pictures/FLPA; 23BL, © Kirsanov/Shutterstock; 23BR, © leungchopan/Shutterstock.

Publisher: Kenn Goin
Creative Director: Spencer Brinker
Photo Researcher: Calcium Creative

Library of Congress Cataloging-in-Publication Data

Gray, Leon, 1974-
 Walking sticks : the world's longest insects / by Leon Gray.
     pages cm. — (Even more supersized!)
 Audience: 6-9.
 Includes bibliographical references and index.
 ISBN 978-1-61772-733-7 (library binding) — ISBN 1-61772-733-4 (library binding)
 1. Stick insects—Juvenile literature. I. Title.
 QL509.5.G725 2013
 595.7'29—dc23

                    2012033457

For more information, write to Bearport Publishing Company, Inc., 45 West 21st Street, Suite 3B, New York, New York 10010. Printed in the United States of America.

10 9 8 7 6 5 4 3 2 1

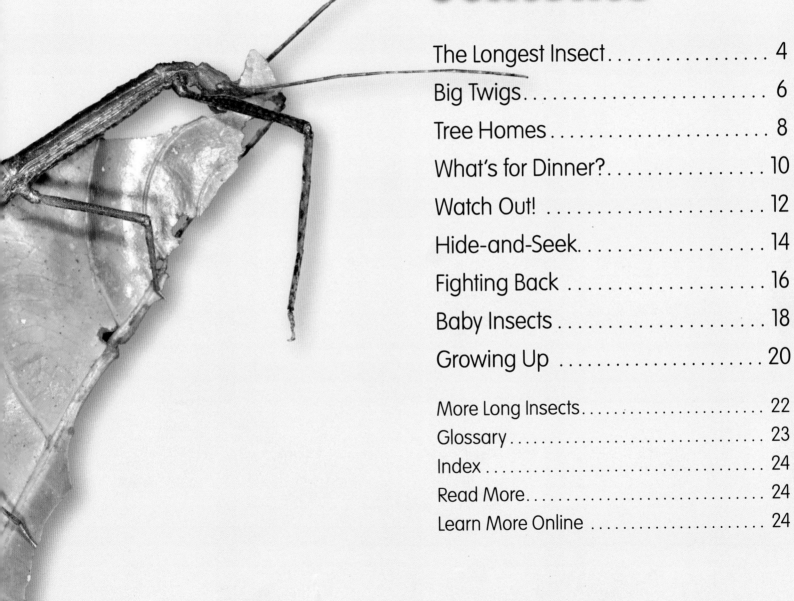

Contents

The Longest Insect

Chan's megastick is the longest **insect** in the world.

It is nearly as long as three new pencils placed end to end.

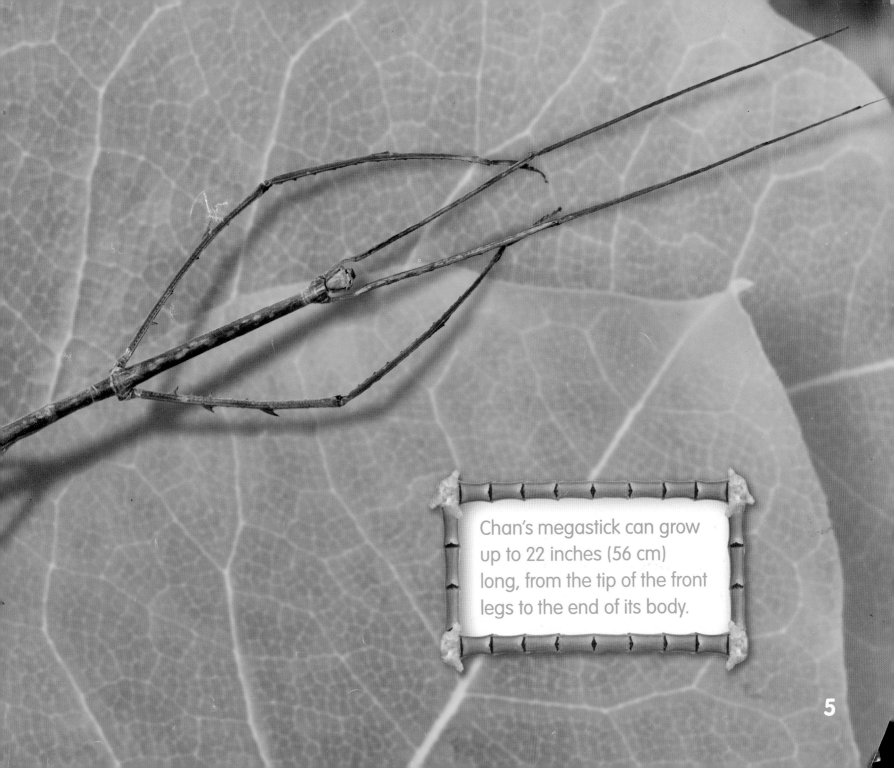

Chan's megastick can grow up to 22 inches (56 cm) long, from the tip of the front legs to the end of its body.

5

Big Twigs

Chan's megastick belongs to a group of insects called walking sticks.

There are more than 3,000 different kinds of walking sticks in the world.

Most of them are between 1.5 and 12 inches (4 and 30 cm) long.

Chan's megastick is the longest walking stick of all.

All walking sticks have thin, twig-like bodies.

Tree Homes

In 1989, a huge walking stick was found in Borneo.

It had been hiding in a tree in a **rain forest**.

An insect collector named Datuk Chan Chew Lun named it Chan's megastick.

The huge insect sleeps during the day, when it is hot in the forest.

It wakes up at night, when the air is cooler, to look for food.

8

Chan's Megastick in the Wild

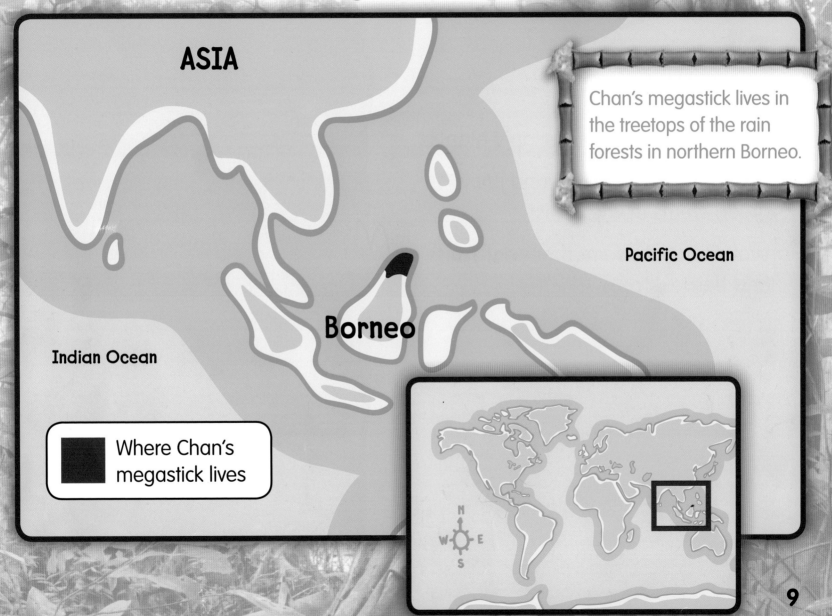

ASIA

Chan's megastick lives in the treetops of the rain forests in northern Borneo.

Pacific Ocean

Borneo

Indian Ocean

Where Chan's megastick lives

What's for Dinner?

Most walking sticks eat only plants.

They munch on leaves and juicy green stems in the forest.

Walking sticks sometimes eat fruits and berries, too.

Some walking sticks spend their whole lives eating and living on one plant. Others walk from plant to plant to find food.

Watch Out!

Chan's megastick is too long for most **predators** to eat.

They cannot fit the huge insect into their mouths!

However, animals such as birds, spiders, and lizards can eat smaller walking sticks.

lizard

white throat

Birds, such as the white throat, are the main predators of small walking sticks.

13

Hide-and-Seek

Walking sticks are usually brown or green.

Their colors and twig-like bodies help them blend in with the trees where they live.

Because they can hide so easily, it's hard for predators to spot them.

walking stick

Some walking sticks rock back and forth as they hide in the trees. This tricks predators into thinking the insects are twigs swaying in the wind.

walking stick

Fighting Back

Walking sticks do not bite, but they will fight back when attacked.

Some walking sticks use spikes on their bodies to poke their enemies.

Others ooze a smelly, bad-tasting liquid when a predator catches them.

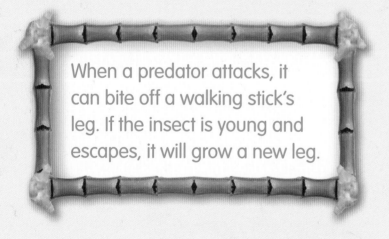

When a predator attacks, it can bite off a walking stick's leg. If the insect is young and escapes, it will grow a new leg.

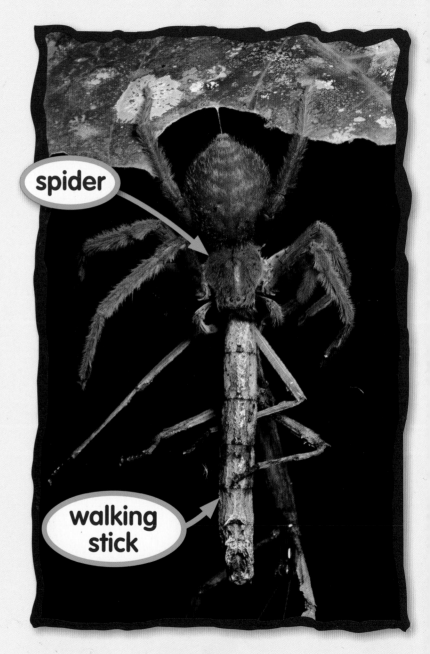

spider

walking stick

Baby Insects

A female Chan's megastick lays eggs that look like small brown seeds.

The baby insects that break out of the eggs are already 2.5 inches (6 cm) long.

The babies are called nymphs.

A megastick nymph looks just like its mother, only smaller.

Chan's megastick egg

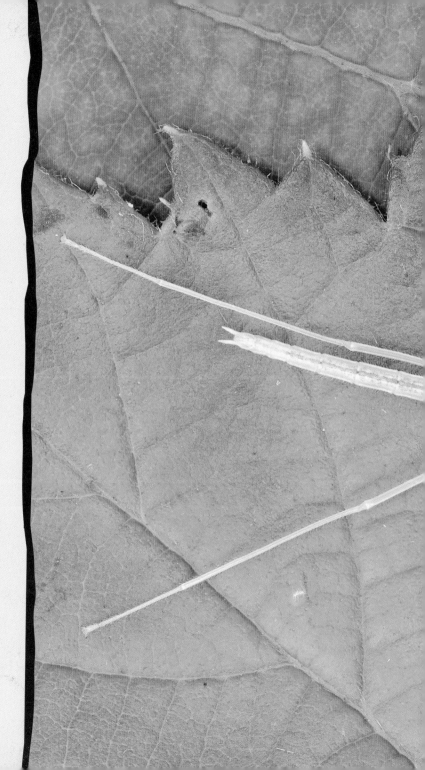

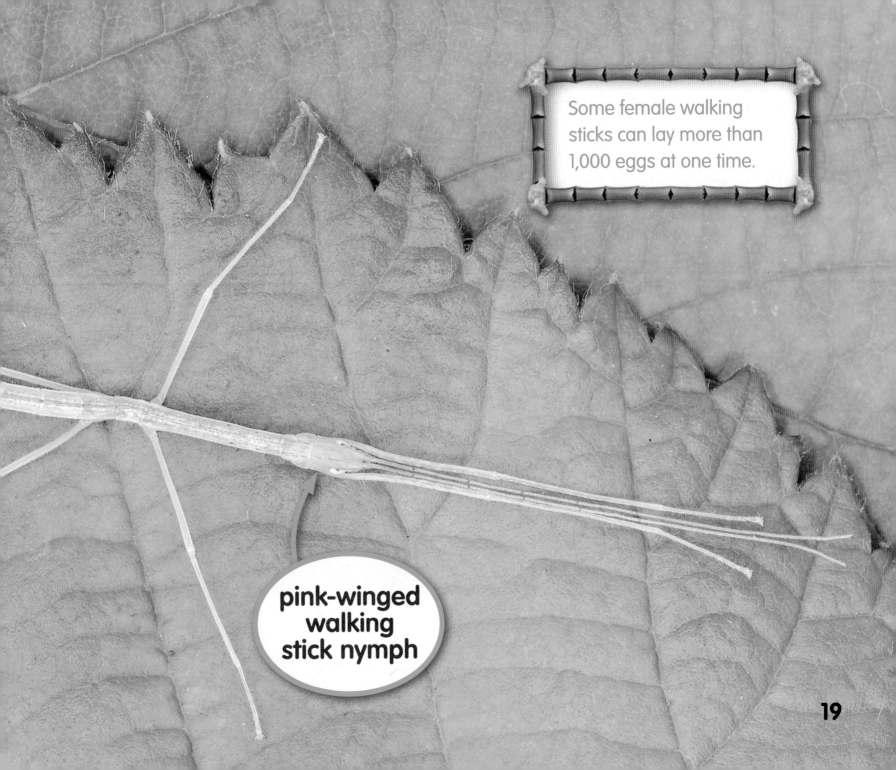

Some female walking sticks can lay more than 1,000 eggs at one time.

pink-winged walking stick nymph

19

Growing Up

A Chan's megastick nymph grows quickly.

The hard **exoskeleton** covering its body soon becomes too small and tight.

As the insect grows, a new exoskeleton forms under the old one.

The walking stick then breaks out of the old exoskeleton, or molts.

A young Chan's megastick molts about ten times before the little insect becomes a big stick.

old exoskeleton

a walking stick molting

an adult Malaysian giant walking stick

It takes about ten months for Chan's megastick to grow to its adult size. Other kinds of walking sticks grow up in just three months.

21

More Long Insects

Walking sticks belong to a group of animals called insects. All insects have six legs and a body that is divided into three main parts. Most insects hatch from eggs. Though almost all insects have wings, some do not.

Here are three more long insects.

Phobaeticus Serratipes

A walking stick called *Phobaeticus serratipes* is the second longest insect in the world. It grows up to 21.6 inches (55 cm) long.

White Witch Moth

The white witch moth from Central and South America has the longest wings of any insect. The wings stretch out more than 12 inches (30 cm).

Titan Beetle

The titan beetle from the Amazon rain forest is the world's longest beetle. Its body can grow to be 6.6 inches (17 cm) long.

Chan's Megastick: 22 inches/56 cm

Phobaeticus Serratipes: 21.6 inches/55 cm

White Witch Moth: 12 inches/30 cm

Titan Beetle: 6.6 inches/17 cm

Glossary

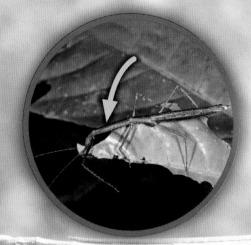

exoskeleton (*eks*-oh-SKEL-uh-tuhn) the hard outer covering of an insect's body

predators (PRED-uh-turs) animals that hunt other animals for food

insect (IN-sekt) a small animal that has six legs, three main body parts, two antennas, and a hard covering called an exoskeleton

rain forest (RAYN FOR-ist) a warm place where many trees grow and lots of rain falls

Index

Read More

Goldish, Meish. *Hidden Walkingsticks (No Backbone! The World of Invertebrates).* New York: Bearport (2008).

Markle, Sandra. *Insects: Biggest! Littlest!* Honesdale, PA: Boyds Mills Press (2009).

Roza, Greg. *Weird Walking Sticks (World of Bugs).* New York: Gareth Stevens (2011).

Learn More Online

To learn more about walking sticks, visit
www.bearportpublishing.com/EvenMoreSuperSized